Our Home

Building A Legacy of Love

Cindy H. Carr, D.Min., MACL

This book is published by **CHC Connect**.

All views and opinions expressed in this work are those of the author. Any errors or omissions are unintentional.

Printed in the United States of America
First Edition, 2025

ISBN: 978-1-971192-08-6

For permissions or inquiries, contact:
Cindy H. Carr
cindyhcarr@outlook.com
www.cindyhcarr.com

Acknowledgments

This book would not exist without the life it came from. To my husband, Dubby, thank you for building this legacy of love with me. Through difference, tension, growth, and grace, you have chosen "us" again and again. Our home is shaped not by perfection, but by persistence, repair, and honoring what God entrusted to us. This book carries the fruit of a marriage lived honestly, imperfectly, and with intention. It meets people in raw searching times.

I am grateful for the wisdom that comes from walking with God. These pages were formed through prayer and Scripture, and the call to love humbly and truthfully. I have also learned from tools and frameworks that translate difference into understanding, reminding us people are not problems to fix, but gifts to steward.

I am mindful of the reach of public words. My hope is to offer something that helps couples stay connected, curious, and committed to building sacred history together. If these pages help even one home choose respect, repair, and love, then this work has done what it was meant to do.

Table of Contents

How to Use This Book

This book is designed to meet you where you are.

Two ways to read:

1) Read + Practice as You Go

After each chapter, you can choose one small step to practice and then turn to The Our Home Tool Kit in the appendix for the scripts, exercises, and plans connected to that theme.

2) Read First, Then Build Your Plan

If you'd rather read the full book first, do that. Let the ideas settle. Then return to the Tool Kit and choose the tools that fit your season. Use it in the order you need—not the order it appears.

A simple weekly rhythm (if you want one):

Read one chapter. Pick one sentence to practice. Do one short "us check-in." Repeat.

Small practices build sacred history.

Introduction: Love Lives Here

I wrote this book because I've watched it happen too many times.

I've seen couples start their journey with true love and real respect—and then, little by little, drift into division. Not all at once. Quietly. One misunderstanding becomes a story. One unspoken expectation becomes distance. Stress becomes tone. Tone becomes contempt.

And I can't tell you how many times I've thought, If someone had walked with them early—if they had been mentored and coached at the beginning—the outcome would have been completely different.

I'm committed to the work of sacred history: helping people build a strong "us." Not a perfect us. A practiced us—one that knows how to reframe before accusing, repair quickly when things get sharp, and keep honor in the room when life gets loud.

This book is for anyone who truly wants to invest the time and effort to build sacred history with someone who is not a cookie cutter of themselves.

Dubby and I married in June 1982, and for more than four decades we've served in ministry and leadership. Along the way, we've watched love grow in ordinary places—at kitchen tables and in hospital rooms—through laughter and loss, routines and surprises. We've learned that it's the small, steady moments that build a life, and the high-pressure moments that reveal what a home is really made of.

Our guidance is not offered from a perfect story but from lessons life has taught us. We've had successes and we've had failures, and all of it has been anchored in the love of God and our commitment to love each other well.

Here's the conviction underneath everything you're about to read: love can be learned. Not just felt—learned. Practiced. Chosen. Trained. Scripture gives us a picture of love that is patient and kind, protective and enduring (1 Corinthians 13). That kind of love doesn't pretend things don't hurt. It refuses to let pain become poison.

A theme runs through this book: difference—different rhythms, needs, stress responses, and ways of giving and receiving love. When we don't understand those differences, we misread each other. We turn personality into accusation and react to assumptions instead of truth.

So we'll practice one skill again and again: reframing. Not to excuse what's wrong or dodge hard conversations, but to stop treating each other like the enemy—so we can tell the truth with love, protect connection, and solve what's real.

In these chapters, you'll learn to lower the heat, name what's happening underneath, and return to love faster. You'll learn courageous, tender communication; wise boundaries without bitterness; quick repair when pressure reveals a shadow; and life-giving words—because what we speak at home either builds safety or breaks it.

Our goal stays the same: a home where love covers, honor is normal, and sacred history keeps growing—one faithful choice at a time.

We begin with vision, not rules. Chapter 1 lays the foundation for what love looks like in real life—and how it becomes the culture of a home. Then we build from there.

Chapter 1: Two People, One Home — God's Good Design for Difference

It did not take long—at all—for Dubby and me to realize we were two totally different people.

At first, that difference felt exciting. It felt like discovery. There was something about the way he saw the world that wasn't like me—and instead of threatening me, it drew me in.

But in those early years, we didn't have the maturity to honor our differences. We only knew how to react to them. And what could have been a gift became friction.

If I'm honest, our first years together weren't great. We had a little bit of fun, yes—but most of what I remember is conflict. We were strong-willed, we both had opinions, and we were quick to slide into the shadow side of ourselves.

By the time our faith became important, we didn't come in as two peaceful people holding hands. We came in with lists—complaint lists about each other. We wanted God to change things. And if we were really honest, we mostly wanted Him to change the other person.

And what breaks my heart now is this: the treasures that drew us together had quickly become the differences that were tearing us apart.

That's why we're starting here. Because difference isn't the enemy.

Difference is part of God's design. He didn't create marriage so two people could become identical—He created it so two people could become united. And unity isn't sameness. Unity is shared direction. Shared commitment. Shared covenant. It's two people learning how to protect one home.

If you don't learn to see each other through God's lens, difference will feel like a threat instead of a gift. You'll start treating the other person's wiring like a problem to fix instead of a person to honor. And you can end up fighting the very thing God meant to use to strengthen you.

At home, unity looks like this: we don't have to prefer the same things to protect each other's dignity. We don't have to process the same way to stay committed to the same "main thing." We can disagree and still be faithful. We can see it differently and still be on the same team.

One of the most powerful shifts in a home is learning to reframe before you accuse. Most families fight about surface behavior, but underneath behavior is usually protection. Someone is protecting order. Someone is protecting rest. Someone is protecting connection. Someone is protecting safety. Someone is protecting dignity.

When you can name what's underneath the moment, you stop attacking the person and you start dealing with what's really happening.

Reframing doesn't excuse sin. It doesn't ignore patterns. It doesn't avoid hard conversations. It just keeps you from turning a moment into a character assassination. It keeps love in the room while you deal with what's real.

Because when difference is seen through God's design, it stops feeling like an obstacle—and starts becoming part of what makes a home strong.

Prayer

Lord, thank You for how You designed me and my spouse. Teach me to honor our differences and keep dignity in the room. Help me see Your design as a gift, not a threat. Amen.

Chapter 2: Assumptions—Misguided Perception

Assumptions are powerful because they feel like facts. When a couple is already tender—when you feel divided, different, and a little raw—you stop experiencing things as neutral. A look has meaning. A pause has meaning. A suggestion has meaning. And before you know it, you're no longer reacting to what happened. You're reacting to what you decided it meant.

In our early years, Dubby and I were especially vulnerable to this. If he offered a suggestion that would genuinely make something easier, my nervous system didn't hear help. I heard critique. My mind translated it into, "He thinks I'm doing it wrong."

My wiring—direct, decisive, ready to act—could also come across as controlling. I wasn't trying to run him. I was trying to move us forward. But his nervous system could hear, "She's taking over."

That's the danger of assumptions: we don't just interpret behavior—we assign motive. And once motive is assigned, the heart reacts.

One of the most helpful shifts for us was learning language for our differences. Frameworks like Myers-Briggs and DISC didn't explain everything, but they helped us stop moralizing difference.

I'm an ESTP and a DI—wired for action, clarity, and forward momentum. Dubby is an ENFP and a C—wired for meaning, care, precision, and doing things well. Neither of us is passive. Neither of us lacks conviction. We simply lead from different centers.

When those differences aren't honored, assumptions rush in.

I can move quickly because I'm confident. He can slow down because he's responsible. If I assume his carefulness is resistance, I start pushing. If he assumes my decisiveness is carelessness, he starts bracing. Two good intentions collide, and the story becomes the problem.

I can speak plainly and efficiently. He is attentive to tone and nuance. If he assumes my directness means I'm against him, he withdraws. If I assume his sensitivity means I can't speak freely, I shut down or sharpen.

I trust correction after movement. He trusts movement after clarity. If I assume he's impossible to please, resentment grows. If he assumes I don't value excellence, anxiety takes over.

What changed everything was this: I stopped turning his carefulness into a character flaw. And he stopped turning my decisiveness into a motive issue. Our differences weren't a problem. Our assumptions about them were.

Repair begins when we slow the story down. When we trade accusation for curiosity. When we ask, "Help me understand what you meant," instead of, "Why would you do that?"

Scripture gives us a simple family leadership plan: be quick to listen, slow to speak, and slow to anger. That isn't a personality trait—it's discipleship.

You don't have to become the same person to become a strong us. Respect doesn't require agreement. It requires curiosity.

Prayer

Lord, I bring You my assumptions and the stories I tell myself. Help me slow down before I assign motive or meaning. Give me humility to clarify instead of accuse, and courage to honor the way You designed my spouse. Amen.

Chapter 3: Unity Isn't Agreement — Staying Connected When You Disagree

One of the clearest places I've seen that unity isn't agreement is with couples who come from different faith backgrounds.

They don't always share the same faith language or the same convictions. And yet I've watched strong couples do something deeply mature: they acknowledge the difference without turning it into a battleground, and they stay united in love and purpose.

Instead of trying to proselytize in their own home—always trying to win—they choose respect. They protect the relationship while they navigate the difference. And that unity becomes an anchor.

Unity isn't sameness. Unity is staying connected while you move forward with honor.

Some families think peace means agreement, so when they disagree, they panic. Other families think strength means winning, so disagreement becomes a contest—who's right, who's wrong, and who's going to give in first.

But there's a better way, and it's the way God teaches us in real life: unity.

Unity is not pretending. Unity is not avoiding. Unity is not forced sameness. Unity is choosing love as the main thing while you work through differences with truth and honor.

One of the most freeing truths God ever taught me is this: unity is not always agreement. If you wait until you see everything the same way, you'll stay stuck. But if you can stay connected while you see it differently, you can grow. And not just grow through the disagreement—you can actually grow closer.

Here's why disagreement can feel so intense at home: it touches belonging. When someone you love sees the world differently, your nervous system can hear it as, "I'm not safe," or "I'm not understood," or "I don't matter." That's why a small conflict about a schedule can turn into a big conflict about respect. The surface issue isn't always the real issue.

Let me describe a familiar moment for a lot of couples.

One spouse wakes up with a plan: errands, chores, a few tasks that have been waiting all week. Their mind relaxes when the list is done. They don't even feel like they can enjoy anything until responsibilities are handled.

The other spouse wakes up, looks out the window, and thinks, *What a beautiful day.* They're imagining a drive with the windows down, a picnic, and unhurried time together. They're not trying to be irresponsible. They're trying to build relationship. Their heart relaxes when connection is nurtured, when the pace slows down enough for laughter, conversation, and presence.

By mid-morning, the task-focused spouse feels anxious: "We're wasting the day if we don't get this done." By mid-morning, the relationship-focused spouse feels dismissed: "We're missing the day—and we're missing each other."

And now the argument isn't really about errands or a picnic. It's about what each person is protecting. One is protecting stability and stewardship. The other is protecting connection and togetherness. Two good desires can collide and still create tension if nobody reframes what's happening.

In a way, it's a modern Mary-and-Martha contrast. One person is trying to care for what needs to be done. The other is trying to care for who needs to be loved. Both matter. And when a couple learns to honor both, they stop fighting over priorities and start building a home that holds responsibility *and* relationship.

This is where unity becomes practical. Unity says, "I'm going to assume there's something good underneath what you want—even if I don't want it the same way." Unity doesn't require you to erase your opinion. It requires you to refuse contempt. It requires you to stay respectful enough to build a plan together.

A simple question can bring people back to partnership: *What is the main thing we both want right now?*

You might both want peace. You might both want a good day. You might both want the kids cared for. You might both want the marriage protected. When you name the main thing, it becomes harder to treat each other as enemies. You're a team again.

And here's another truth that brings relief: not every disagreement requires full agreement to move forward. Sometimes what you need is understanding. Sometimes you need compromise. Sometimes you need to take turns. Sometimes you need to say, "We don't see it the same, but we're committed to each other, and we will not punish each other for having a different lens."

Scripture gives us wisdom for this. Romans teaches us to "live at peace with everyone" as far as it depends on us (Romans 12:18, NIV). At home, that doesn't mean you swallow everything. It means you stay truthful without becoming cruel. It means you refuse contempt. It means you keep the relationship more sacred than your pride.

So let me offer a simple pattern that keeps disagreement from turning into distance. Start by naming the good you see. Then name your need without accusation. Then ask for a plan—not a win.

When you do that, you stop debating motives and start building something workable. And over time, unity stops being a concept you admire and becomes a culture you live.

Prayer

Lord, thank You that unity does not require sameness. Help me love with respect when we see things differently. Anchor us in shared purpose and keep us connected in honor. Teach me to listen well and to protect our "us." Amen.

Chapter 4: Love Languages and Love Lenses — We Say "I Love You" Differently

One of the biggest breakthrough moments in our marriage came through Gary Chapman's book *The 5 Love Languages.*

For a long time, I couldn't figure out why we were missing each other so much. We loved each other. We were trying. And still, it often felt like we weren't connecting.

What I didn't understand at first was this: Dubby was expressing love constantly—but he was expressing it the way he most naturally felt loved. And I was doing the same. The problem wasn't effort. The problem was translation. We were saying "I love you," but we weren't always saying it in a way the other person could truly hear.

So we kept giving our partner what *we* wanted our partner to give us. And for a while, we couldn't understand why it wasn't working.

Once we recognized the difference and started meeting the other person's need on purpose, it was a game changer. Love can be sincere and still miss its target—until you learn what actually builds connection for the person in front of you.

One of the most surprising things about marriage and family life is this: you can be loving—and still not feel loved.

Not because love isn't there, but because connection isn't forming in the way the other person needs most.

A lot of us assume the people closest to us should just know. We think *I'm doing my best—how can you not see that?* But love doesn't always translate automatically. It has to be shown in a way that connects with the other person

And here's the other piece most people don't realize at first: this isn't a one-time conversation. Learning connection is a process. People grow. Seasons change. Stress shifts needs. What makes someone feel loved in one chapter of life may not be what they need in the next. That's why healthy homes keep learning each other—without shame, without defensiveness, and without assuming you "should already know."

Here's the truth: people don't just want love. They want love that feels personal, love that sees them.

And when someone gives love in a way that doesn't match your wiring, it's easy to misread it as absence.

Sometimes one person shows love by doing—fixing, providing, handling tasks, making sure life works. That is love. It's care with sleeves rolled up. But the other person may feel loved most through presence—unhurried time, conversation, attention, warmth. They don't just want help. They want you.

Sometimes one person shows love through words—encouragement, affirmation, reassurance. The other feels love most through follow-through—consistency, action, effort. They're not trying to be difficult. They're wired to feel safe when love is steady and practical.

Sometimes one person feels loved through touch and closeness. The other feels loved through respect and space. And if you don't name the difference, you can start interpreting space as rejection, or closeness as pressure, when it might simply be different needs in the same home.

None of this means anyone is wrong. It means you're different. It means you have lanes. And when you don't name the lanes, you'll tend to personalize the difference.

Let me give you a simple example. One spouse plans something sweet—a gift, a reservation, a thoughtful surprise. They're trying. They're reaching. They want to bless. The other spouse receives it kindly, but still feels disconnected—not because they're ungrateful, but because what they needed wasn't a gift. They needed conversation. They needed time. They needed presence.

Then the gift-giver feels unappreciated: "Nothing I do is enough." And the other person feels unseen: "They don't really know me." And just like that, both people are trying—and still missing each other.

Scripture gives us the posture we need here. Love is patient and kind (1 Corinthians 13:4, NIV). In family life, patience often looks like slowing down long enough to learn the other person. Kindness often looks like refusing to take it personally while you're still learning what helps love connect.

I also want to say this gently: sometimes what you need now is connected to what you lacked before. A person who grew up unseen may crave presence. A person who grew up criticized may crave encouragement. A person who grew up unsafe may crave predictability. A person who carried too much may crave help.

That doesn't mean your spouse or child is responsible for healing your whole story. It just means love needs gentleness. You don't shame someone for what they need. You learn them. And you ask God to help you love with wisdom.

The goal isn't to label everybody in your house. The goal is to become more intentional—to stop missing each other in good intentions, and to love in ways that actually build connection.

One simple habit can help, especially if you feel like you're passing each other in life: a small daily reconnect. It doesn't have to be deep. It just has to be real.

Take five minutes. No speeches. No fixing.

"How did I love you well today?"
"What would help us connect better tomorrow?"

Then end with one sentence of gratitude—small is fine. Over time, this removes guessing, softens tension, and gives love a target.

Prayer

Lord, teach me to love my spouse in the way they most need to receive love. Show me where I've been loving sincerely but missing the mark. Give me attentiveness in the small moments—words, time, touch, help, presence. Help me practice love on purpose, not only when it feels easy. Let connection grow in our home in a way that feels seen and steady. Amen.

Chapter 5: Shadow Under Pressure — What Shows Up When We Feel Threatened

Even in a good marriage, stress has a way of pulling your shadow self out of the closet. You can love each other deeply, be committed, and be doing a lot of things right—and still find yourselves snapping, withdrawing, or getting tense when the day has worn you down.

One pattern we had to recognize was what happened when we came home. We were carrying so much stress from the day, and we weren't really processing any of it. So instead of leaving it out there, we brought it right into the house with us. More than once, we thought we were upset with each other, when the truth was we were often just upset with the day—and our home became the place it spilled.

What we needed wasn't another argument. We needed a simple way to unload the weight and reconnect. For us, it looked like a quick debrief: "What was hard today?" so the other person could offer support, and "What was good today?" so we could celebrate together. That small shift changed the atmosphere, because it gave the stress somewhere to go besides onto each other. And here's the line that still helps me: don't make your spouse pay for what your day did to you.

The truth is, most of us don't meet the worst version of ourselves on our best day. We meet that version when we're hungry, tired, overwhelmed, under-resourced, or emotionally tapped out. We meet it when we feel threatened—when something inside us feels exposed, dismissed, misunderstood, or out of control. Pressure doesn't create a brand-new person; it usually just pulls forward the parts of us that show up when we don't feel safe.

That's why family life can feel so intense. Home is where we relax, but it's also where we're most unguarded. It's where the "public version" of us can finally sit down, and the parts of us that have been holding it together all day can surface. That's also why I want to be very clear: this chapter isn't here to shame you. It's here to help you recognize your patterns sooner, so you can repair faster and keep love in the room.

When I use the word *shadow* in this book, I'm simply naming what shows up when you don't feel safe, or when you don't feel strong. It's the reactive version of you—the one that snaps, withdraws, over-controls, over-talks, gets sharp, goes cold, shuts down, escalates, or starts keeping score. And what's important to understand is that under pressure, your strengths don't disappear. They often get exaggerated. A strength without love can turn into a shadow.

You've probably seen this in real time. A person who's naturally responsible can become controlling when they're scared. A person who's naturally peaceful can become avoidant when they're overwhelmed. A person who's naturally discerning can become critical when they're hurt. A person who's naturally helpful can become resentful when they've been carrying too much for too long. Most of us rotate through more than one pattern, but we usually have a default. And once you can name your default, you stop being surprised by yourself—and you stop feeling helpless in the moment.

In many homes, four shadow patterns show up again and again, and you can usually spot your default pretty quickly once you know what you're looking for. Some people tighten the grip. They manage, correct, press for clarity, insist on order—not always because they're mean, but because something in them is trying to protect stability, dignity, or a fear of failure. Others withdraw. They go quiet, disappear into a screen, shut down emotionally, or avoid the conversation—not always because they don't care, but because they're trying to protect peace, avoid overload, or prevent escalation.

Some people get sharp. They point out what's wrong, become sarcastic, use tone as a weapon, critique instead of connect—not always because they hate you, but because they're trying to protect standards, self-worth, or an old wound that just got touched. And some people over-function. They fix, rescue, carry everything, and then quietly resent everyone for not noticing—not always because they want control, but because they're trying to protect others from discomfort, or protect the home from falling apart.

Once you see your pattern, the next step isn't condemnation—it's curiosity. Because most shadow behavior is protection behavior. It's what we do when we don't know how to ask for what we need in a clean way. That's why one question can be so helpful when you feel yourself getting defensive: What am I trying to protect right now? It might be your rest, your peace, your role, your competence, your dignity, your hope, your sense of control, or maybe a fear of being blamed or unseen. When you can name what you're protecting, you can choose a better response than reaction.

Let me describe a moment that shows up in some form in almost every home. It's the end of a long day. Dinner is halfway done. A child is asking questions. Someone is running late. The counter is a mess. Your body is tired and your mind is crowded. In that moment, one spouse may be trying to protect order—"Can we please just get through this evening without chaos?"—while the other spouse is trying to protect connection—"Can we not turn the whole house into a stress zone?"

Usually it doesn't start with something big. It starts with one sentence that comes out sharper than it should. Then another. And suddenly you can feel the air change. Everybody's nervous system is on alert, and you can almost watch the room shift from calm to tense. In that moment, most families go one of two directions: escalation or repair.

And this is where I want to give you real hope: repair is a skill, not a personality trait. Some people grew up in homes where repair never happened. Conflict just lingered, or everybody pretended, or someone exploded and then moved on like it didn't matter. So if you didn't learn repair, it doesn't mean you're doomed. It simply means you're learning it now.

Quick repair doesn't mean you pretend nothing happened. It means you don't let love bleed out while you figure it out. Most of the time, repair looks like a few simple moves done with humility. You name the break without blame—because you can feel when the room shifts, and it helps to say it out loud: "That landed sharp," or "I can feel the tension rising." Then you own your part without turning it into a speech: "I'm stressed and I spoke harshly. I'm sorry." And then you reconnect with a plan, even a small one: "Can we reset?" "What do we need right now?" "Give me ten minutes and I'll come back calmer." That's how you protect the relationship while you solve the problem.

Now let me name one danger signal clearly, because it does real damage if it becomes normal: contempt. Eye-rolling. Mocking. Sarcasm meant to cut. Name-calling. The tone that says, "You're beneath me." Contempt doesn't just express frustration—it attacks dignity. And dignity is the soil love grows in.

If contempt has started to feel normal in your home, don't despair, but don't minimize it either. Take it seriously as information. It's a sign the culture needs a reset, and you may need help rebuilding a safer way to communicate. There is no shame in that. Protecting your home is wise stewardship.

Prayer

Father, when pressure rises, help me notice my shadow before it spills into my home. Teach me to bring You the weight of my day instead of placing it on my spouse. Guard my tone. Slow my reactions. Soften my words. Help us debrief, support, and celebrate each other so we stay on the same side. Make our home a refuge where love is safe—even on hard days. Amen.

Chapter 6: Reframing for Connection

One of my favorite things is watching what happens when reframing finally clicks for a couple. People get together because they truly love one another, but they drift apart because assumptions take over—"I'm working harder," "I'm alone," "You don't care." And once those assumptions settle in, it doesn't take much for everyday moments to start feeling personal.

But when we sit down across a table and work through reframing tools, you can almost see reconnection happen in real time. A couple that felt distanced starts understanding again—and once they understand, they can see a clear path back.

That's why I teach reframing as a way of life. It's like a kitchen tool: if you're going to cook on the stove, you pull out the skillet—every time. In the same way, when you feel the drift, you reach for the tool and say, "Wait. We need to stay connected. Let's reframe this."

Most families don't need bigger feelings. They need better language. When we don't have words for what we're experiencing, we tend to default to two options: we explode or we retreat. We either come in too hot, or we disappear. And then later we wonder why the conversation didn't go well.

Words matter at home because home is where your nervous system is already tender. It's where you're tired, unguarded, carrying responsibilities, and trying to feel safe with the people you love most. That's why the smallest sentence can either calm the room—or set it on fire. So let me say this plainly: the goal is not to win a conversation. The goal is to keep love in the room while you tell the truth.

That's what reframing really is. It's not denying what happened, and it's not pretending you don't feel what you feel. Reframing is learning how to slow down the story your emotions want to tell and speak from a better frame—one that protects dignity and keeps the relationship intact. A reframe doesn't erase the moment; it changes how you carry it. And that one shift can turn a fight into a conversation.

So here are a few reframing tools you can keep in your pocket—not as scripts you have to memorize, but as simple ways to stay honest without becoming harsh.

When a conversation is tense, one of the strongest things you can do is name the good first. Not because you're pretending everything is fine, but because it reminds both of you that you're not enemies. You might say, "I know you're trying to do what's right," or "I know you care about our home," or "I can see you're protecting something important." When you start there, defensiveness drops. People soften when they feel seen.

Another reframe that changes the temperature is separating intent from impact. In families, we can get stuck arguing about intent: "That's not what I meant." But even when intent was good, impact can still be real. So you might say, "I believe you didn't mean to hurt me—and it still landed hard," or "I know you weren't trying to dismiss me—and I felt dismissed." That keeps the conversation from turning into a courtroom. It also makes room for empathy without denying the truth.

Then comes the part most people skip: naming your need cleanly. Needs are not accusations. Needs are information. And healthy homes learn to speak needs without shame. That can sound like, "I need a calmer tone," or "I need a plan," or "I need ten minutes of connection before we jump into tasks," or "I need help carrying the load this week." The moment you say a need clearly, you give the other person something they can actually respond to.

From there, it helps to reframe the goal. Most conflict gets ugly when the goal becomes winning. A better goal is partnership, which means you move the conversation toward a plan. You can ask, "What would a plan look like that protects both of us?" or "What can we agree on for today?" Those questions take you out of debate mode and back into teamwork.

And when you realize your tone has drifted—because it will sometimes—the most mature thing you can do is repair quickly. Not later. Not tomorrow. Right then, when you feel it. A repair phrase is not weakness. It's leadership. It can sound like, "That came out sharper than I meant," or "I'm sorry—let me try again," or "I'm overwhelmed, but I'm not against you." Those phrases are small, but they protect the atmosphere of your home.

One more thing—and I want to be honest with you: sometimes you'll be the only one practicing this. Don't let that discourage you. One person who stays anchored can change the temperature of a whole room. It doesn't fix everything, but it can soften hearts and make room for change.

Reframing helps you lead with honor, but it doesn't mean you ignore what's unhealthy. If disrespect is ongoing—sarcasm, contempt, intimidation, or cruelty—that's not a "communication style." That's information. Wise people pay attention to information and let it guide their next steps. Love and wisdom belong together.

Prayer

Lord, when I feel the drift, remind me to reach for reframing instead of blame. Help me slow down and seek understanding. Give us language that turns heat into honor and distance into connection. Teach us to protect our "us" and return to unity quickly. Amen.

Chapter 7: Communication — Speak for Connection and the Common Goal

One of the most life-changing gifts I've been given came from my precious mentor, Wendy J. Miller, when I was at Eastern Mennonite Seminary.

She taught me the skill of active listening. And I say *skill* on purpose—because listening isn't a personality trait. Every person can learn it. You can break the habit of interrupting, and you can break the habit of preparing your response while someone is still talking.

Communication is one of the top reasons relationships fail, and that's why it's worth the effort to train for it—like you would train for any job you want to do well. This is the relationship you live in 24/7. Learning to listen is not optional. It is one of the most loving skills you can bring into your home.

If there is one skill that can change a home faster than almost anything else, it's communication. Not perfect communication. Not therapy-level vocabulary. Just communication that stays inside honor—especially when emotions are high.

Most tension at home isn't caused by a lack of love. It's caused by mixed signals, unspoken expectations, and words that land harder than we meant them to. That's why two people can love each other deeply and still feel like they're constantly missing each other. Communication is the bridge that turns "me and you" back into "us."

One reason good people still clash is because they're speaking from different lanes. One person talks to think; the other needs time to think before they talk. One person is direct; the other is gentle. One person needs details; the other needs the main thing. None of that is wrong—it's wiring. But when wiring isn't honored, it gets misread. Direct becomes "rude." Gentle becomes "weak." Silence becomes "punishing." Words become "controlling." And suddenly you're not solving the issue—you're debating each other's character.

So let me give you a reframe that keeps communication clean: before you talk about the problem, name the shared goal. Ask, "What do we both want right now?" You might both want peace. You might both want a plan. You might both want to feel respected. You might both want connection. You might both want your home to feel steady. When you name the shared goal, you stop making each other the enemy and start acting like partners again.

Here's another truth that saves families a lot of pain: sometimes the issue isn't what you're saying—it's when you're saying it. Timing is a strategy for healthy communication. If someone is hungry, exhausted, overstimulated, coming off a hard day, or walking in the door with a full nervous system, they may not have capacity for a complex conversation. That doesn't mean the issue doesn't matter. It means wisdom matters.

One mature sentence can protect connection: "I want to talk about this, but not like this. When can we come back to it?" That sentence is not avoidance. It's leadership.

A simple pattern also helps people feel safe enough to stay in the conversation. You don't need a speech—you need a clean rhythm. Start with honor and name what you see that is good. Then name impact in one sentence. Name need in one sentence. And finally, ask for partnership as you move toward a plan. That keeps you out of the courtroom. Families don't need winning arguments; they need workable agreements.

And because communication is not only speaking—it's also listening—let me give you something that builds trust quickly: reflect before you respond. Not to perform. Not to sound impressive. Just to make sure the other person feels heard. You can say, "What I hear you saying is ___." Then ask, "Did I get that right?" and "Is there anything else you want me to understand?"

Reflecting isn't agreeing. It's honoring the person by taking them seriously. It's saying, "You matter enough for me to slow down."

Over time, healthy communication creates something families desperately need: clarity. Most homes don't need a thousand rules. They need a few clear agreements—about tone, repair, responsibilities, and how decisions get made. When communication is clean, agreements stop feeling like control and start feeling like care.

And when you miss it—because you will sometimes—the most important thing is not defending yourself. It's repairing quickly. A home becomes safe when repair becomes normal.

Prayer

Lord, teach me to listen the way You listen—present and patient. Break my habit of interrupting and preparing my defense. Help me hear the heart beneath the words and respond with respect. Give me courage to speak truth without heat and humility to admit when I'm wrong. Let our communication be a place where trust grows and tenderness returns. Amen.

Chapter 8: Parenting Lenses — Two Styles, One Team

Parenting gets complicated fast when you have two parents with two different styles, and it gets even more layered because every child you add brings another lens into the home. Each child comes with their own personality, their own wiring, and their own needs. In a real way, we're co-creators with God as we shape and steward each child He entrusts to us. We're on a journey to discover and develop the design God "baked in." And sometimes, without meaning to, we can hinder what God placed there when we try to make a child's personality fit our narrative instead of learning who they actually are.

Some of the strongest leaders were the most energetic kids. Yes, some children need extra support, but most need interaction. That's why it can feel so hard when you come home tired and your energizer bunny needs you—because interaction is hard when you're tired, and it's still the job.

Parenting also has a way of exposing everything in a marriage. You can be deeply committed to your children and still clash constantly—not because either of you is careless, but because you're looking at the same child through different lenses. And when you're tired, stressed, or carrying a lot, those different lenses can start feeling personal.

In our home, this was real. My parenting style was more relational. My instinct was often, *why say no if yes will do?* Dubby's style was more structured, clear boundaries, clear expectations. And that difference created some explosions in our house.

Looking back, we both wish we had been mature enough to appreciate how each of us was wired and then bring the best of both strengths to our children. There were times we did. But life happens—and when pressure rises, many couples don't blend their strengths. They fight against each other's design.

This chapter isn't about shame. It's about wisdom. Because the goal isn't for one parent to "win" and the other to "give in." The goal is to become one team.

Here's why parenting differences feel so intense: they don't feel like preferences. They feel like values. One spouse may be protecting safety and long-term character. The other may be protecting connection and emotional health. And if you're not careful, you start turning those lenses into accusations: "You're too soft," or "You're too harsh."

But underneath those labels are usually two frightened prayers. One sounds like, "I don't want our child harmed." The other sounds like, "I don't want our child hardened." And if you can hear the prayer underneath the parenting style, you can stop fighting each other and start fighting for your child together.

Scripture holds both warmth and wisdom. It speaks of training and instruction, and it also speaks of gentleness and not provoking. Ephesians 6:4 tells parents not to exasperate their children, but to bring them up with training and instruction (NIV). That verse doesn't pick a side—it calls us to balance: guidance without harshness, discipline without humiliation, structure without emotional shutdown.

One of the most important shifts a couple can make is deciding, *We're not going to undermine each other in front of the kids.* When parents contradict each other in front of children, kids may not say it out loud, but they feel it: *If mom and dad aren't together, I'm not safe.* That doesn't mean you never adjust course. It means you do it privately whenever possible, and you come back with unity.

And if your home has had tense moments around parenting, let me offer you hope: it's never too late to change the atmosphere. Repair works. Growth is possible. You can reframe how you see each other and become partners again.

The gentle lens often protects connection, emotional safety, and a child's sense of being seen. The structured lens often protects boundaries, responsibility, and long-term formation. When those two lenses honor each other, children gain both—warmth and wisdom, compassion and clarity.

And because this is real life, I want to name a moment that still hits me hard. I'll never forget my oldest daughter praying one day as we were fighting in the kitchen. I asked what she was doing, and she said, "I'm praying that you and daddy will stop fighting."

That is a gut punch. And if you've had a moment like that, you know: our kids don't just hear our words. They feel our atmosphere.

The good news is you can change that atmosphere. Not overnight, maybe—but truly. And one of the strongest ways to begin is to stop treating each other like the obstacle and start treating each other like your teammate.

Prayer

Father, thank You for the children You've entrusted to us. Help me honor my spouse's parenting lens and not turn difference into accusation. Give me wisdom to see who our child is—how You wired them—and to steward that well. When I'm tired, strengthen me to stay present and choose connection on purpose. Unify us as a team. Give our children the gift of peace at home.

Chapter 9: Money, Time, and Capacity — The Big Three Family Friction Points

This chapter is critical. I could write a whole book on money. I could write a whole book on time. But if I had to choose the strongest point here—especially for marriage—it would be this: you have to love your spouse enough to pay attention to their capacity.

Not everybody's capacity is equally matched. Some people are made to carry a lot. Others have a smaller capacity—and that doesn't mean they're weak. It just means their bandwidth, recovery time, and stress tolerance are different. And capacity isn't permanent, either. It changes by season. What you could carry last year might not be what you can carry right now, and wise families learn how to adjust without shame.

This is where relationships can start to feel lopsided. But it isn't fair for a person to live in a relationship where they are constantly not measuring up. Capacity isn't a character issue. It's a stewardship issue. When couples honor capacity, they stop blaming each other for being human and start building plans that fit real life.

If you want to predict where most families will argue, you don't need a crystal ball. You just need a calendar and a bank statement. Money, time, and capacity are the big three—not because families are shallow, but because these three areas reveal what we value, what we fear, and what we believe we can carry. And when one of these starts to feel shaky, people don't just get practical—they get emotional. That's when tone shifts. That's when assumptions rise. That's when small decisions start feeling personal.

Most couples aren't fighting because they don't love each other. They're fighting because, somewhere underneath the surface, someone doesn't feel safe. So here's the reframe that changes these conversations: instead of asking, "Why are you like that?" ask, "What are you trying to protect?"

Money: stewardship or security?

Money fights are rarely just about dollars. They're about meaning. One person may relate to money as stewardship: *We need a plan.* Another person may relate to money as security: *We need to feel okay.* Both of those matter. The problem comes when one person frames planning as control, or the other person frames spending as irresponsibility.

In real homes, money often reveals different "lanes." Some people feel peace when there's a budget and a clear path forward. Some people feel peace when everyone's needs are met and responsibilities are carried. Some people feel peace when they can be generous and respond to real needs. Some people feel peace when there's margin and the future feels protected. Some people feel peace when life is enjoyed and money doesn't become a prison.

And here's where this gets practical, because these differences show up in predictable places: what counts as "too much" to spend without talking first, how you handle subscriptions and small recurring costs, how quickly you want to pay off debt, how much cushion you want in savings, and what generosity looks like in your home. These aren't just financial decisions—they're emotional ones, because each choice touches security, freedom, stewardship, or joy.

None of those lanes are automatically wrong. But any lane can turn into fear. And fear will always demand a fight—unless you reframe the conversation and name what each person is protecting. A money reframe sounds like, "I'm not against you. I'm trying to protect our future," or "I'm not trying to be careless. I'm trying to protect joy and peace." When you hear the heart underneath the habit, you stop villainizing each other and you start building a plan.

Time: structure or connection?

Time is the invisible budget of a home. When time feels scarce, tension rises quickly. Some people feel safer with structure—schedules, routines, and predictability because it lowers their stress. Other people feel safer with connection—unhurried moments, conversation, flexibility—because that lowers their stress.

If you don't reframe those differences, the structure person can start thinking the connection person is irresponsible, and the connection person can start thinking the structure person is controlling. Both interpretations can be wrong at the same time.

You can usually spot this conflict in the first hour after work, in weekends, and in transitions. One person wants a plan so the day doesn't get away from them; the other wants space to breathe so life doesn't feel like a schedule. Even good things—family time, rest, ministry, friendships—can become tension points when time feels thin and nobody names what they're trying to protect. That's why so many fights happen around weekends, evenings, and "right when we walk in the door." It's not just logistics—it's what time means to each person.

Capacity: how much can we carry?

Capacity is your emotional, physical, and mental margin—and capacity issues usually show up as tone issues. One spouse may be maxed out from work. Another may be maxed out from caregiving. Kids can be maxed out from school pressure, social pressure, or their own internal world. When capacity is low, even simple requests can feel like threats. And when you feel threatened, your shadow shows up faster.

That's why one of the most honest and helpful things a family can say is, "Here's what I have capacity for this week—and here's what I don't." This isn't lowering standards. It's telling the truth so you can build a plan that actually works in real life.

Let me describe a common collision. It's Sunday night. One spouse wants to plan the week—calendar, meals, appointments, kid schedules, money decisions. The other spouse wants to decompress. Their week has been heavy, and what they need most is quiet.

If you're not careful, the planner interprets quiet as avoidance, and the decompressor interprets planning as pressure. And suddenly the fight isn't really about planning—it's about what each person is trying to protect. One is protecting stability. One is protecting rest. If you can name that, you can build a plan instead of repeating a pattern.

Sometimes the plan is simple: "Can we take 15 minutes now to handle essentials, and then we rest?" That kind of agreement protects both lanes.

Scripture is practical about this balance. Proverbs honors wise planning—"The plans of the diligent lead to profit" (Proverbs 21:5, NIV). But Scripture also speaks to the weight of anxiety and overload—"An anxious heart weighs a man down" (Proverbs 12:25, NIV). Healthy homes learn to plan without anxiety and rest without avoidance.

The two-lens approach that works in all three areas

Whenever money, time, or capacity gets tense, here's a simple way back to each other. Start by naming what each person is protecting. Then name what each person needs—in one clean sentence. From there, build a plan that honors both lanes, keeping it small and specific. And finally, choose a review time—because plans get better with practice, and seasons change.

Prayer

Lord, help me love my spouse with attention to their capacity. Show me where I've pushed past what we can carry or treated limits like a character flaw. Teach us to plan with humility, simplify when needed, and honor each other's wiring. Help us build rhythms that fit our season—financially, emotionally, and spiritually. Provide what we need and give us peace in wise choices. Amen.

Chapter 10: Clean Conflict — How to Fight Fair and Repair Fast

This chapter—fighting fair—is close to my heart, because every family fights. The question isn't whether you'll have conflict; the question is whether your conflict will be clean or corrosive. Clean conflict protects dignity. Corrosive conflict attacks it. And over time, whatever happens most often becomes the culture of the home. That's why this chapter matters—not because the goal is to avoid hard conversations, but because the goal is to have them in a way that keeps love alive.

I've seen this especially when one spouse has a strong speaking gift and the other has a strong serving gift. The articulate spouse can dissect with words, and without meaning to, can dominate the room. The serving spouse can start to feel like they can never win, never get the final word, never be heard—and eventually they stop trying. If you are excellent with words, love requires restraint. You have to make space to hear what the other person is trying to say. The goal isn't to win the argument. The goal is to be the safest place. If your words can cut, your love has to teach your words to slow down.

Here's a simple reframe that changes everything: not all conflict is the same. Some conflict is problem conflict—a practical issue needs a decision. Money, schedule, chores, parenting, boundaries, responsibilities. Problem conflict needs a plan. Other conflict is pain conflict—a wound has been touched. Feeling unseen. Feeling disrespected. Feeling afraid. Feeling ashamed. Feeling alone. Pain conflict doesn't just need a plan; it needs presence, empathy, and repair. When you treat pain conflict like a problem conflict, people get louder and more stuck. When you treat problem conflict like pain conflict, nothing gets resolved. Learning to tell the difference keeps you from talking past each other.

Now, if you want to keep conflict clean, you also have to recognize the "dirty moves" that poison a home quickly. These moves don't just express frustration—they create fear, because they attack safety and dignity.

One common dirty move is global language: "You always…" "You never…" It turns one moment into a lifetime verdict, and nobody feels safe under a verdict. Another dirty move is character attacks: "You're selfish." "You're controlling." "You're lazy." Those words don't correct behavior; they attack identity. And once identity is attacked, the nervous system goes to war instead of staying present.

Another dirty move is contempt—sarcasm meant to cut, mocking, eye-rolling, name-calling, the tone that says, "You're beneath me." Contempt is especially dangerous because it doesn't just disagree; it devalues. And dignity is the soil love grows in.

And then there's what I call the courtroom—dragging in old cases, unrelated issues, third-party conversations, and past failures. The courtroom overwhelms the moment and turns the conversation into a trial instead of a repair. If you catch any of these showing up in your mouth, don't power through. That's your cue to pause and reset. You don't have to be perfect—you just have to be willing to repair.

So what does clean conflict look like in real life? It isn't fancy. It's honest, and it stays inside honor. One simple rhythm can keep you out of the courtroom and bring you back to partnership: you begin by anchoring the relationship, then you speak the truth, then you build a plan.

That can sound like this: start by naming the good you can genuinely see, because it reminds both of you that you're not enemies. Then name impact with one clear sentence—what happened and how it landed. Then name your need without accusation. Then ask for partnership by moving toward a plan.

And if your tone drifts (because it will sometimes), repair quickly—right then—before the issue grows teeth. That rhythm doesn't deny conflict; it keeps conflict from becoming cruelty.

Let me show you how it changes a common fight. One spouse is exhausted and says, "You don't help." The other spouse hears a character attack and responds, "I do help! Nothing I do is enough." Heat rises, voices rise, and now you're fighting about identity instead of building a plan.

A clean version sounds different: "I know you work hard, and I'm overwhelmed. I need a plan for the next seven days so the load is shared." That doesn't deny the frustration—it directs it toward something workable. It keeps love in the room while you deal with what's real.

Jesus gives us practical wisdom about conflict. Matthew 18 teaches us to go directly to the person involved rather than recruiting allies (Matthew 18:15, NIV). In a family, that means we don't build camps. We don't vent to the kids. We don't triangulate. We talk to each other—with honor.

And as much as possible, we don't let breaks sit and rot. In many homes, silence becomes punishment and distance becomes normal. But a healthier norm is simple: repair quickly—within 24 hours when possible. Scripture even speaks to this kind of urgency: "Do not let the sun go down while you are still angry" (Ephesians 4:26). That doesn't mean every problem is fully solved by bedtime; it means we don't let anger harden into distance. Love matters more than pride, and connection is worth protecting.

Repair can be short. It can be one sentence of ownership and one sentence of connection: "I'm sorry for my tone. I love you. I'm committed to working this out." That kind of repair doesn't excuse the issue—it keeps the relationship safe while you work on it.

Sometimes you do need a timeout, and timeouts can be wise when they're used with honor. A timeout isn't a punishment; it's regulation. It's a way to calm the nervous system so you can come back and speak like someone who loves their family. The key is that a healthy timeout includes a return time. Not disappearing. Not slamming a door. Not cold silence. A return time and a commitment to come back kinder. That's how you protect both truth and tenderness.

Prayer

Lord, guard my words when conflict rises. Keep me from scoring points or dominating the room. Teach me to listen deeply, speak with honor, and repair quickly. Make our home the safest place for truth and the quickest place for mercy. Amen.

Chapter 11: Boundaries Without Bitterness — Especially With Extended Family

Boundaries matter because a lot of the friction in a marriage doesn't actually come from within the relationship—it comes from without. Work demands, extended family, enmeshment, expectations, and outside voices can pull on a marriage until the "us" gets thin. And when the "us" is thin, it doesn't take much to create tension at home.

For me, one of the clearest signals that a boundary is being crossed is what I call the "yucky gut"—that irritation I can feel in my body. Over time, I've learned to treat that feeling like information. It's my boundary check, and when it shows up I ask myself: am I giving someone more access than I can handle? Am I giving them more space in my head than they should have? Or am I watching someone take more of my partner than our home can carry?

Because if you don't set boundaries lovingly, resentment will set them for you.

One of the hardest places to keep "us" strong is extended family, because you're not just dealing with relationships—you're dealing with history. Roles. Expectations. Old patterns. Unspoken rules. And if you grew up in a strong loyalty culture, you may even feel guilty for thinking about the word *boundary* in the first place.

But boundaries are not rejection. Boundaries are wisdom.

A healthy boundary is simply a line that protects what God has entrusted to you. It protects love, responsibility, and the peace of your home. It tells the truth about what you can carry and what you cannot, and it helps you stay connected without living constantly pressured, resentful, or overextended.

For some people, boundaries can feel unspiritual. They've been taught that love means unlimited access—if you say no, you're selfish; if you protect your space, you're unkind. But Scripture doesn't ask you to become a doormat. Jesus loved people deeply, and He also withdrew, said no, refused manipulation, and didn't let other people's expectations drive His calling. Healthy families learn to do both: love well and lead wisely.

Here's a reframe that helps a lot of people: every boundary is actually a yes. When you say no to one thing, you're saying yes to something you're responsible for—yes to your marriage, yes to your children's stability, yes to your peace and capacity, yes to rest, yes to integrity, and yes to the culture you're building in your home. That's why boundaries aren't about control. They're about stewardship.

You see this most clearly around holidays, events, and family expectations. Every holiday, the pressure rises. One side expects everyone all day, and the other side expects the same. A couple feels torn—if they choose one, the other feels rejected, and if they try to do both, they're exhausted and the kids melt down. And when the couple is worn down, resentment rises fast. A boundary doesn't instantly fix everyone's emotions, but it does create a plan that protects your home. Sometimes it sounds as simple as, "We love you. This year we're doing lunch with you and dinner at home. Next year we'll rotate."

Most extended-family boundaries tend to fall into a few categories. There are time boundaries—how long, how often, what days, and what rhythm you can realistically sustain. There are emotional boundaries—what tone is acceptable, what conversations go nowhere, what topics become toxic, and what you will no longer keep revisiting.

And there are access boundaries—what decisions belong to you, what roles belong to you, and what input is invited (and what isn't).

Boundaries also become much easier to hold when they include two things at the same time: warmth and clarity. Warmth sounds like, "We love you," "You matter to us," and "We want to stay connected." Clarity sounds like, "Here's what we can do," "Here's what we can't do," and "Here's what will happen if the tone crosses a line." A lot of people struggle here because they try to keep the peace by being vague. But vagueness creates confusion, and confusion creates repeat conflict. Clarity is kindness when it's paired with love.

And yes—sometimes people will push back. The truth is, people often resist boundaries because they were benefiting from your lack of boundaries. Pushback doesn't automatically mean your boundary is wrong. It may simply mean your boundary is new. You don't have to explain forever, and you don't have to get mean in order to be firm. You can be kind and steady at the same time.

Now let me speak to an even harder reality, because it matters: sometimes reconciliation isn't possible yet. That word *yet* is important, because it keeps hope alive without pretending the hurt has stopped.

If the same cycle keeps repeating—if there's no ownership, only excuses, blame-shifting, or minimizing—if there's no willingness to change or accept accountability, and if you feel unsafe emotionally or physically (or your children are being impacted), then you may need stronger boundaries for a season.

You can keep a lens of honor without denying the truth. You don't have to demonize someone to be wise. You can say, "I want healing, and I'm willing to rebuild—when the pattern changes."

And I want to say this clearly: if you or your children are not safe, get immediate help from trusted local support—a counselor, pastor, advocate, or emergency services. Safety is not a lack of faith. It's wise stewardship.

Prayer

Lord, give me wisdom to set boundaries with love and without bitterness. Help me recognize irritation as information and respond with clarity, not resentment. Protect our marriage from outside friction and misplaced expectations. Give me courage to say no when needed and grace to stay kind while holding the line. Strengthen our "us" and keep our home steady. Amen.

Recommended Resource (Optional)

If you want a deeper guide to boundaries (especially guilt, pushback, and clarity), see: Cloud, H., & Townsend, J. (2017). *Boundaries: When to say yes, how to say no to take control of your life* (Updated & expanded ed.). Zondervan.

Chapter 12: Forgiveness and Trust — Rebuild Without Pretending

Forgiveness is one of the most misunderstood words in family life, and a lot of that confusion comes from the mixed messages people have heard over the years. Some think forgiveness means pretending it didn't happen. Others think it means you're supposed to instantly feel close again. And many people assume forgiveness and reconciliation are the same thing—so if you forgive, you're expected to "move on" as if nothing changed.

But in real homes, we need a mature, practical understanding of how this actually works. Here's the clearest way I know to say it: forgiveness is releasing the debt, and trust is rebuilding the relationship. Those two things are connected, but they don't always move at the same speed. That isn't cold. That's wisdom.

Scripture calls us to forgive from the heart (Matthew 18:21–22, NIV), and Scripture also teaches discernment. Proverbs is full of wisdom about what is safe, what is true, and what patterns produce fruit. Forgiveness doesn't cancel wisdom—it strengthens it. You can forgive and still require change before closeness.

One reframe that helps people breathe is this: forgiveness is a heart decision between you and God, but trust is a relationship process that has to be rebuilt with consistency. When you confuse forgiveness with trust, you can end up reopening doors that still need boundaries. That's why it helps to name it clearly and stop putting pressure on yourself to treat two different processes like they're the same thing.

So what *is* forgiveness? Forgiveness is releasing the right to punish. It's refusing to rehearse bitterness as a lifestyle. It's handing the case to God. It's choosing, when possible, to bless rather than curse, and refusing to let poison become your personality.

And just as important—what is forgiveness *not*? Forgiveness is not saying it didn't matter. It's not calling harm "no big deal." It's not forcing immediate access. It's not skipping boundaries. Forgiveness doesn't erase consequences; it keeps consequences from turning into hatred.

This is where many families get stuck: an apology happens, but trust still feels shaky. Someone says, "I'm sorry—can we move on?" And the hurt person often *wants* to move on, but their body doesn't trust it yet. The pattern has repeated too many times.

They're not trying to punish; they're trying to protect what's sacred.

A wiser way forward is to separate the two processes. Forgiveness can be immediate. Trust is paced. Sometimes the most loving and truthful sentence is simple and steady: "Thank you for apologizing. I forgive you. And for trust to rebuild, I need to see consistency over time."

Because trust isn't rebuilt by big speeches. Trust is rebuilt by repeated, small integrity—over and over—until something new becomes normal.

In real homes, you can usually tell trust is rebuilding when a few markers start showing up consistently. First, there's ownership—real ownership that names what happened without excuses, blame-shifting, or minimizing. Then there's change—not vague promises, but specific adjustment: "Here's what I'm doing differently." After that comes consistency—the change shows up again and again, especially when it's inconvenient. And finally, there's repair—when someone misses it, they repair quickly instead of defending. They don't act offended that you're still tender. They stay accountable.

Now let's talk about the hardest scenario: forgiving someone who won't change. This is where many people need permission to be both merciful and wise. You can forgive in your heart and still keep distance. You can release bitterness and still maintain boundaries. You can love and still not give full access to someone who repeatedly harms.

Here's a sentence that helps a lot of people hold both truths at once: forgiveness frees you from carrying poison, but boundaries protect you from drinking it again.

And if the conflict is inside your home—your spouse, or a family member living with you—trust rebuilding often requires agreements. Agreements are not punishment. They're protection. They don't shame people; they protect peace and dignity while growth happens. That can sound like, "If voices rise, we take a timeout and come back," or "If sarcasm shows up, we stop and reset." It may sound like, "If a boundary is crossed, we pause access until repair happens," or, in practical situations, "If something is broken, it gets repaired or replaced." Healthy agreements give everyone a clear path forward—and they reduce the fear that nothing is going to change.

I also want to share a tender part of our story here—not to be dramatic, but to make this chapter real.

Early in our marriage, we walked through a painful loss that left me carrying more grief than I knew how to name. In that season, I coped poorly. I pulled away, I numbed out, and I made a choice that broke trust: a one-night affair.

There is no explaining that away. Betrayal is a real wound. But here is what I want you to know: we did love each other, and when the truth came into the light, we chose a path of repair.

Dubby gave me one of the greatest gifts of our marriage. He didn't excuse what happened, and he didn't shame me into the ground. He chose mercy with integrity. He said something like, "If Jesus says that lust in the heart makes us guilty, then I'm not standing above you. Let's walk forward together."

That is what "love covers a multitude of sins" looks like in real life (1 Peter 4:8). Covering is not hiding. Covering is protecting dignity while telling the truth. It's refusing to weaponize a failure while still doing the work of rebuilding trust—step by honest step.

If your story includes betrayal, I want to honor you. Sometimes repair is possible, and sometimes it isn't possible yet. In either case, God can lead you one faithful step at a time.

Prayer

Lord, teach me to forgive as You have forgiven me. Give me humility to own my part and courage to tell the truth. Help us rebuild trust with wisdom and patience, not pressure. Heal what has been wounded and restore what can be restored. Amen.

Chapter 13: Space Without Distance — Supporting Individual Wiring While Staying Connected

When two people come together to form an inseparable union, the two do not become one in the sense that they cease to exist. In a healthy marriage, it becomes three: two individuals and one team. That means respect and honor have to remain rooted in the individuality of the people making up the team. Marriage shouldn't cancel what makes you *you*—your passions, your hobbies, and the things that restore you.

In our home, that has looked very practical. Dubby loves fishing, so we make space for it on purpose. Every year we pull out the calendar and look at tournament schedules before we plan family vacations. That isn't fishing over family. That's family honoring what resets him and brings him back to us with energy and joy.

Some of the healthiest families I know have learned something simple: you don't have to do everything together to stay connected. In fact, one of the most loving things you can do in a home is make room for each person's wiring—without turning that space into distance, withdrawal, or "fine, do your thing." Space can be a gift when it's paired with connection. It becomes a way of saying, "I want you to stay alive inside yourself—and I'm staying with you while you do."

I'm not talking about separating a family. I'm talking about learning how to support one another's rhythms, interests, and callings without making anyone feel punished for having them. Because here's what happens when a person feels like they have to shrink, numb out, or abandon what energizes them just to keep peace at home: resentment grows quietly. But when a person feels supported to be themselves—and supported to carry responsibility too—joy grows. A home becomes stronger not by forcing sameness, but by learning how to honor difference with mature teamwork.

This played out in our family in a very specific way. When tournament season came, fishing required time—long days, early mornings, focus, energy. In the early years, that difference could have become a fight. You can probably hear it: "Why do you get to go do what you love while I'm stuck with everything else?" But instead of letting it turn into a tug-of-war, we learned to trade support.

When Dubby was on the water, I covered the home lane so he could be fully present where he was. And just as important, there were plenty of things I loved to go and do. When it was my turn, he covered the home lane so I could be fully present in what energized me. That rhythm didn't weaken our family—it strengthened us. It taught us that love is not only affection; it's coverage. It's teamwork. It's saying, "I've got the house so you can go be the person God made you to be."

But let me say this clearly: space only stays healthy when it's paired with clarity and care. Healthy space is not avoidance. It's not silent punishment. It's not "I'll do my life and you do yours." It's not disappearing without explanation and then acting confused when your spouse feels alone.

Healthy space sounds like clarity: "Here's where I'm going, here's how long, and here's what needs covered." And it sounds like care: "I'm coming back to you. I'm for you. I'm for us."

A lot of tension around "space" isn't really about space—it's about feeling abandoned, overloaded, or left holding the whole home while someone else gets to breathe. If one person's energizing lane consistently costs the other person exhaustion, the lane isn't the problem—the plan is. The goal is mutual support, not one-sided freedom.

Here's a fair question that keeps a home honest: What do you need covered so we can both be alive and responsible? When couples can talk that way, space stops feeling threatening and starts feeling like teamwork.

And if you want to make space feel safe instead of confusing, one small practice helps a lot: name the reconnection point. It can be as simple as, "I'm be gone for a few hours. When I get back, I want ten minutes with you before we jump into anything else." That sentence tells your spouse, "You still matter. I'm not drifting away. I'm coming back to you."

Prayer

Lord, thank You for the unique wiring You placed in each of us. Help me honor my spouse's passions without turning space into distance. Give us fairness, clarity, and teamwork so both of us can thrive and still belong. Teach us to reconnect on purpose and to cover each other with love. Amen.

Chapter 14: Creating "Us" — Family Agreements That Hold Under Pressure

Creating "us" is personal. It's intimate. Outsiders looking in will misjudge and try to insert who they are into your relationship—and that guidance will often be wrong for your home. You don't need a marriage that looks like someone else's. You need a marriage that is healthy, honest, and faithful for the two of you.

In our house, we've always had two strong leaders. We're opinionated, and our discussions can be loud. But in our loud discussions, we're still connected. We aren't dividing—we're debating. That's our wiring, and we've learned not to interpret intensity as disunity.

Here's one of our core agreements: we don't move until we have one answer—until we agree on the right decision. Most decisions can wait for agreement, and we've learned that waiting is often wiser than forcing a fast answer that leaves one person feeling unheard.

When something can't wait, we trust the lane. I handle finances. He handles home maintenance. So if there's a roof leak and I'm thinking it's not a good financial time, but he's the one constantly plugging leaks, I have to submit to reality: now is the time. That isn't me losing. That's me trusting my team.

A strong family doesn't happen by accident. It happens by intention. And intention doesn't mean perfection—it means you decide what kind of home you're building, and you keep returning to that decision. Because every home has a culture. The only question is whether the culture is intentional or accidental.

If you want to stop "us vs. them" inside your own house, you need a shared "us." You need something you both come back to when emotions rise and life gets loud. And that "us" is built through agreements—small, repeated choices that become normal.

Joshua said it like this: "As for me and my household, we will serve the Lord" (Joshua 24:15, NIV). That verse isn't just about being religious. It's about being intentional. It's a decision: this home will have a center. And when God is the center, honor becomes normal. Repair becomes normal. Mercy becomes normal. Truth becomes normal. When life presses on you, you don't have to invent who you are in the moment—you return to what you've already agreed on.

Here's an important reframe: a family agreement is not a rule to control people. It's a shared promise that protects relationships. It's how you say, "This is how we do life together." It becomes a guardrail that helps you stay loving when you're tired, stressed, disappointed, or stretched thin.

The strongest agreements tend to be simple—one sentence, positive, and clear enough that you can tell whether it's happening. They're also repairable, meaning when you miss it, you don't spiral into shame or blame; you reset and come back. Over time, agreements become the emotional language of your home, and they shorten the distance between tension and repair.

Let me make this practical. A couple is tired. The kids are loud. Dinner is late. The whole room feels edgy. Someone starts to snap and you can feel an old pattern about to take over. In that moment, the home doesn't need a long speech. It needs a simple return point. One spouse says, "No contempt in this house. Let's reset." That's it—no sermon, no shaming—just a shared agreement that calls everyone back to the culture.

That's what agreements do. They keep the atmosphere from drifting, and they keep the home from becoming a battlefield.

Here are a few agreements you can borrow and adjust to your family's voice. You don't need all of these at once—you just need a few that fit your home right now, agreements that feel like a yes to what you're building:

We honor each other's dignity. No contempt in this house.
We reframe before we accuse.
We name needs without shame.
We repair quickly when we miss it.
We protect rest and capacity. We don't glorify burnout.
We solve problems as a team. No camps. No triangulation.
We celebrate differences as part of God's design.

And here's the piece that makes agreements stick: rituals. Agreements are the words. Rituals are the practice. A weekly "three budgets" check-in—time, money, and capacity. A nightly five-minute reconnect. A repair phrase you actually use. A gratitude moment at dinner or bedtime. A small weekly fun anchor—something that reminds everyone, "We're more than our stress."

When you have older kids or adult children, “us” shifts. Your posture moves from control to connection. But agreements still matter, especially around tone, honesty, respect, and repair. You’re not building compliance; you’re building relationship and responsibility.

Prayer

Lord, help us build an “us” that is protected and intentional. Quiet outside voices that don’t fit our covenant and guide us into what’s best for our home. Give us humility to listen, courage to speak, and patience to wait for agreement. Teach us to trust the lanes You’ve given us and decide with unity and honor. Make our agreements strong enough to hold when life gets loud. Amen.

Chapter 15: Legacy at Home — The Culture You Hand Down

To build a legacy of love is to build sacred history. Sacred history means you prioritize what will matter long after this moment passes. You choose the relationship over the temporary issue, and you refuse to let something temporary become the culture of your home.

And sacred history almost always comes back to capacity. Many families keep doing what they've always done without reading the room—without noticing that one partner no longer has the capacity to carry it. Love pays attention, and love adjusts.

Until 2015, we opened our home consistently to people in transition—coming out of jail, walking through divorce, needing a refuge to regroup. It was rewarding, holy work. But in 2015, our capacity shifted and we had to stop, because we needed our home to be a refuge for our family again.

That was hard. It was hard when people reached out expecting our doors to be open and felt hurt when we said no. I tried to be vulnerable and honest: there had been a season when we could do that, but with where we were in life, we could no longer. I would pray for them, and if I could guide them somewhere else, I did. But sometimes all I could offer was prayer.

Capacity shifts. Seasons change. Love doesn't disappear when capacity changes—it changes form. And sometimes prayer is not the smallest thing you can offer. It's the truest thing. That is part of how you guard the sacred union and build a legacy that lasts a lifetime.

Whether you mean to or not, every home is building a legacy. Not just a legacy of money, photos, holidays, or the things people can post, but a legacy of atmosphere—the kind of home your family becomes inside of, the emotional weather that settles over a kitchen, a living room, a car ride, a Saturday morning.

Because the truth is, your children—and everyone who lives under your roof—are learning what love feels like. They're learning what conflict looks like, what respect sounds like, what safety feels like, and what "normal" is. Legacy isn't only what you teach; legacy is what you normalize.

And the good news is this: if you don't like what has become normal, you can change it. Not by becoming perfect, but by becoming intentional.

When children become adults, they may not remember every rule, but they remember how the house felt. They remember whether they had to brace for tone, whether conflict got repaired or just went quiet, whether they felt seen or overlooked, and whether love felt steady or conditional. That's legacy.

Scripture gives us a picture of what love looks like in a real community, not just in a wedding ceremony. Love is patient. Love is kind. It does not keep a record of wrongs (1 Corinthians 13:4–5, NIV). That isn't sentimental—it's a description of culture.

In a home, patience often looks like slowing down enough to understand. Kindness often looks like protecting dignity even when you're frustrated. And "keeping no record" doesn't mean ignoring patterns; it means you don't use old failures as weapons.

So if you want to build a legacy that blesses the people who live in your house, focus on a few simple things. Not complicated. Not heavy. Just faithful.

First, protect the way you speak. Homes drift into "us vs. them" when labels become normal: "You're lazy." "You're dramatic." "You're controlling." "You're too sensitive." Labels might feel like relief in the moment, but they damage dignity over time—and dignity is the soil love grows in. A healthier legacy is learning to reframe instead of label. That doesn't mean you never correct; it means you correct behavior without attacking identity.

Instead of, "You don't care," you learn to say, "I'm feeling alone, and I need connection." Instead of, "You're controlling," you learn to say, "I think you're protecting stability." Instead of, "You're too sensitive," you learn to say, "That landed hard. I want to understand." That kind of language builds a house where people can be human and still be safe.

Second, make quick repair normal. In many families, the strongest person in the room is not the loudest; it's the one who can say, "I was wrong." Quick repair doesn't require long speeches—it requires humility. It sounds like, "That came out wrong. I'm sorry," or "I raised my voice. That wasn't love," or "I made you the enemy, and I don't want that."

When kids see adults repair, they learn that relationships are strong enough to handle truth. They learn that love is sturdy. They learn that you don't have to pretend. You can tell the truth and come back to each other.

Third, keep a few shared agreements. Agreements are family guardrails. They keep your home from drifting back into old patterns when life gets loud. Agreements like: no contempt, quick repair, shared load, truth without heat, rest matters, and we don't undermine each other. Over time, agreements become identity. They become, "This is who we are." And that kind of clarity is a gift in a family.

And finally, build joy on purpose. A lot of families are faithful, responsible, and exhausted. They're doing the right things, but joy feels rare—and when joy gets rare, everything gets heavier than it needs to be. Joy is not a luxury in a home. Joy is fuel. It reminds a family: we are more than our schedules and responsibilities. We are loved people building a life together.

Joy can be small: a weekly dessert night, music while cooking, a walk after dinner, a "funny moment of the week" at the table, or a no-agenda Saturday morning once a month. It doesn't have to be expensive. It just has to be intentional.

Here's what happens when a family chooses even a few small resets: the home changes. Not because life gets easier, but because the family gets stronger. Not because nobody struggles, but because struggle no longer becomes the atmosphere. That's legacy—small choices repeated until they become culture.

Prayer

Lord, help me build sacred history in my home. Teach me to choose the long-term over the temporary and love over being right. When our capacity shifts, give me courage to adjust without guilt and compassion without resentment. Help us steward our marriage, our family, and our calling with wisdom. Let our legacy be love that lasts—a steady "us" that reflects You. Amen.

Epilogue: Not Me and Them — Us

If you take nothing else from this book, take this: difference is not the enemy. Disrespect is the enemy. Contempt is the enemy. Pride is the enemy.

Difference is often part of God's design. And when you learn to honor it instead of weaponize it, it can become a gift in your home—not because it's always easy, but because God can use it to help your family grow stronger, wiser, and more connected.

God designed your family on purpose. He didn't accidentally place different people under one roof and then hope you figured it out. He gave you the capacity to grow, He gave you grace, and He gave you Himself—because we do not build healthy homes by willpower alone. We build them by staying connected to the God who created us and learning to treat each other like His workmanship—"very good."

So when tension rises this week, come back to what you already know. Reframe before you accuse. Name the good before you name the issue. Speak your need without shame. Ask for a plan, not a verdict. Repair quickly when tone drifts. Protect your home with wise boundaries. Build joy on purpose.

And when you miss it—and you will sometimes—don't quit. Don't let shame write the ending. Repair. Return. Try again.

Healthy families aren't the ones who never struggle. They're the ones who refuse to let struggle become the culture. They refuse to let stress turn them into enemies, and they refuse to let the hardest season become the loudest voice in the house.

You are building something holy and practical at the same time: a home where people can be human, grow strong, and learn love that lasts.

Not Me and Them — Us.

A Final Blessing

May the Lord give your home peace that's practical, love that's courageous, and joy that's steady. May your words be life-giving, your boundaries be wise, and your repairs be quick. May your family reflect the heart of God in everyday ways. Amen.

Appendix: The Our Home Tool Kit

You don't need more information—you need language you can actually use when life gets loud. This Tool Kit gathers the practical scripts, reframes, check-ins, and exercises from the book in one place. Use it after each chapter or after you finish the book—whatever best serves your home.

Chapter 1

- Where does "us vs. them" show up most in your home (money, time, parenting, chores, tone, planning, extended family)?
- What recurring difference are you tempted to take personally?
- How could that difference be part of God's design—not a flaw?
- What reframe sentence will you practice once this week?
- What one agreement will you try for the next 7 days?

Chapter 2

- In what area do assumptions show up most (tone, timing, texting, chores, money, parenting, planning)?

- What is one assumption you've been treating like a fact?
- What "blank" do you tend to fill in when you feel hurt or stressed?
- What question could you ask instead of concluding?
- Where will you practice slowing down once this week?

Chapter 3

- Where do you most often disagree (time, money, parenting, pace, roles, extended family, tone)?
- What good are you trying to protect in that disagreement?
- What good might your spouse be trying to protect?
- What would a "both-and" plan look like for the next 7 days (not forever)?
- What would respectful unity look like even if full agreement isn't reached?

Chapter 4

- What is your most natural way of giving love?
- What is your most natural way of receiving love?

- Where have you misread someone's love because it didn't match your wiring?
- What one small action would help love land better this week?
- What question can you ask daily that keeps connection current (not assumed)?

Chapter 5

- What is your default shadow pattern under stress (control, withdraw, criticize, rescue)?
- What are you usually trying to protect when it shows up?
- What is one replacement response you'll practice this week?
- What repair phrase do you want to normalize in your home?
- What boundary around timeouts would keep them honorable (return time, tone reset, re-entry)?

Chapter 6

- Under stress, do you drift toward explosion or retreat?
- What need do you struggle to say clearly (without apologizing or accusing)?

- What "dirty move" shows up most when you're activated (tone, sarcasm, shutting down, defensiveness)?
- What reframe line will you use the next time tension rises?
- What quick repair phrase will you practice immediately when tone drifts?

Chapter 7

- When conflict hits, what pattern shows up first (silence, sarcasm, over-talking, defensiveness, shutting down)?
- What does your spouse most need from you to stay in the conversation (tone, time, clarity, gentleness, space)?
- What do you want your spouse to understand about you—and can you say it in one sentence?
- What timing adjustment would reduce repeat conflict this week?
- What one agreement would make communication feel safer this month?

Chapter 8

- What is your natural parenting lens (more relational/gentle or more structured/clear)?

- What good are you trying to protect with that lens?
- What good is your spouse trying to protect that you can honor?
- Where are you most likely to undermine each other—and what plan will prevent it?
- What one parenting issue needs a "two-lens huddle" this week?

Chapter 9

- Which creates the most tension right now: money, time, or capacity?
- What is each person trying to protect in that area?
- What is one small agreement that would reduce stress this week?
- What does "plan without anxiety" look like in your home right now?
- What does "rest without avoidance" look like in your home right now?

Chapter 10

- What "dirty move" shows up most under stress (always/never, character attacks, contempt, courtroom)?
- What would clean conflict look like this week—one specific change?

- What repair phrase will you use the moment you notice tone drift?
- Is there a conversation you've been avoiding? What is the first clean step?
- What would it mean to aim for repair within 24 hours in your home?

Chapter 11

- Where does outside pressure strain your "us" most (holidays, time, money, parenting, opinions, control)?
- What boundary would protect love and responsibility in that area?
- What warm-and-clear sentence will you use (write it out)?
- Where do you need to "decide together first" before talking to others?
- What consequence/limit would you hold if the tone crosses the line?

Chapter 12

- Where do you most need forgiveness right now—toward someone else or toward yourself?
- Where do you need to separate forgiveness (heart release) from trust (rebuilding)?

- What one specific change would rebuild trust in this relationship?
- What boundary would prevent repeating the same harm?
- What timeline/check-in would make trust rebuilding feel real (30/60/90 days)?

Chapter 13

- What energizes you—and have you made room for it without guilt?
- What energizes your spouse—and have you honored it lately?
- Where does "space" get interpreted as rejection in your home?
- What would a fair coverage plan look like this week (who covers what, when)?
- What reconnection point would help space feel safe?

Chapter 14

- If your home had a motto, what would you want it to be (one sentence)?
- What agreement does your family need most right now (tone, contempt, repair, load, rest, unity)?
- What ritual would make that agreement real this week?

- What difference have you treated as a threat that could become a gift?
- What would "returning to us" sound like when emotions rise?

Chapter 15

- What three words describe your home's atmosphere right now?
- What three words do you want to describe it a year from now?
- What is one pattern you want to stop handing down?
- What is one practice you want to start handing down?
- What would "joy on purpose" look like in one simple plan this month?

About the Author

Cindy H. Carr, D.Min., MACL, has spent decades helping people build healthier lives, stronger relationships, and communities of care. She has served in ministry since 1986, walking alongside individuals and families through transition, grief, restoration, and growth.

Cindy and her husband, Dubby, have been married since 1982. Together they have built a life marked by faith, perseverance, and history that comes from real life: joy and sorrow, success and failure, side by side.

They live openly because healing grows when people feel less alone. By sharing their marriage and family story, the wins and wounds, they remind couples: you can grow, rebuild and move forward. This "glass house" vulnerability helps others build steadier homes with real hope.

With coaching language, practical tools, and Scripture woven in, Cindy helps couples protect connection, honor differences, and build a home where love can thrive for generations.

Connect with Cindy: CindyHCarr.com

www.ingramcontent.com/pod-product-compliance
Lightning Source LLC
LaVergne TN
LVHW011047110826
845149LV00015B/3393

9781971192086